WHAT IS ART?

Drawings and Cartoons

KAREN HOSACK

CHICAGO, ILLINOIS

Editorial: Adam Miller, Charlotte Guillain, Clare Lewis,
and Catherine Veitch
Design: Victoria Bevan and AMR Design Ltd
Illustrations: David Woodroffe
Picture Research: Mica Brancic
and Helen Reilly/Arnos Design Ltd
Production: Victoria Fitzgerald

Originated by Modern Age
Printed and bound by CTPS (China Translation and
Printing Services Ltd)

12 11 10 09 08
10 9 8 7 6 5 4 3 2 1

Library of Congress Cataloging-in-Publication Data
Hosack, Karen.
  Drawings and cartoons / Karen Hosack.
    p. cm. -- (What is art?)
  Includes bibliographical references and index.
  ISBN 978-1-4109-3163-4 (hc)
  1. Drawing--Juvenile literature. 2. Cartooning--
Juvenile literature. I. Title.
  NC50.H67 2008
  741--dc22
                                        2008009684

Acknowledgments
The publishers would like to thank the folllowing for
permission to reproduce photographs: © AD Ltd
pp. **20**, **21**; © AKG Images p. **13**; © Arnos Design
Ltd p. **12**, **17**; © Alamy pp. **24** (Chris Wilson), **25**
(Jupiter Images/Agence Images); © Art Resource NY
(Photo Resource/Yale University Art Gallery) p. **7**; ©
Bridgeman Art Library pp. **5** (© Succession H. Matisse/
DACS 2008), **9** (© Succession Picasso/DACS 2008),
11 (Bibliotheque des Arts Decoratifs, Paris, France,
Archives Charmet), **14** (Victoria & Albert Museum,
London, UK), **15** (National Gallery), **27** (Museum of
Fine Arts, Houston, Texas, USA, Funds provided by
the Alice Pratt Brown Museum Fund); © The Trustees
of the British Museum p. **4**; © www.Cartoonstock.com
p. **19**; © Getty Images p. **23** (Sebastian Willnow); ©
Scala/Art Resource pp. **6**, **10**; © The Art Archive p. **8**
(Erich Lessing); © The National Gallery, London p. **16**;
© The Royal Collection p. **26**; © Vintage Magazines
Archives pp. **18**, **22**.

Cover photograph of "Cartoon Monsters" reproduced
with permission of © Picture Hooked/Si Clark.

Every effort has been made to contact copyright
holders of any material reproduced in this book.
Any omissions will be rectified in subsequent
printings if notice is given to the publishers.

Disclaimer
All the Internet addresses (URLs) given in this book
were valid at time of going to press. However, due
to the dynamic nature of the Internet, some addresses
may have changed, or sites may have changed or
ceased to exist since publication. While the author
and publishers regret any inconvenience this may
cause readers, no responsibility for any such changes
can be accepted by either the author or the publishers.
It is recommended that adults supervise children
on the Internet.

Contents

What Is Drawing?..4

Making Drawings More 3-D..............................6

Drawing as a Discipline..............................8

Art and Science..10

Tricks of the Trade..............................12

Research Drawings..............................14

What Are Cartoons?..............................16

Cartoons Today..18

Famous Cartoonists..............................20

Comic Books and TV Cartoons..............................22

Drawing on Walls..............................24

Drawing Conclusions..............................26

Timeline..28

Where to See Drawings..............................29

Glossary..30

Learn More..31

Index..32

Any words appearing in the text in bold, **like this**,
are explained in the glossary.

What Is Drawing?

One of the first things artists learn is how to draw. Drawing is the starting point for most works of art and, in some cases, the final piece as well. In this book we are going to look at some very famous drawings, different ways of drawing, and reasons why some artists prefer to draw rather than paint, sculpt, or take photographs.

This drawing was made by the artist Michelangelo in preparation for his painting on the ceiling of the Sistine Chapel in Rome, Italy. This was a huge project that he started in 1508. He would have made many hundreds of drawings similar to this one. Michelangelo drew the figures using a **model** in front of him. This is called drawing from life.

Michelangelo drew using a model so that he could see exactly what happens to a body when it twists and turns.

Study for *The Last Judgment* by Michelangelo Buonarroti, c. 1540

Ballet Dancer by Henri Matisse, 1949

Both Henri Matisse and Michelangelo used a method of drawing called **sketching**. This is when artists use small feather-like lines to describe what they are looking at. By using small lines that are at first lightly drawn, artists are able to make their drawings very accurate.

Making Drawings More 3-D

To make drawings look **three-dimensional** (3-D), artists use **shading**. Drawings with shading are called **tonal** drawings and can make a flat shape appear more life-like. Here the artist has used a technique called **cross-hatching**. He has drawn small lines in one direction and then drawn others over the top in another direction.

Studies of Heads and Arms by Baccio Bandinelli, c. 1545

When there are more layers of cross-hatching, then the tone is darker. When the lines are wider apart, then the tones are lighter.

Artists can also create tone using dark and light drawing materials. In this drawing the dark tone is charcoal, which is burned wood. The light shades are the blank paper and chalk.

Seated Boy with Straw Hat, Study for *Bathers at Asnières* by Georges Seurat, 1883

Light

Artists need to know where to put the dark and light shades as they draw. To do this they decide where the light source is coming from. The light source could be the sun, an electric lamp, or a window. Artists notice where the light shines on an object and put the lightest tones there. They see where the object is in shadow and put the dark shades there.

Drawing as a Discipline

Most artists practice drawing regularly as a **discipline**. This means that artists are always trying to improve their drawing skills or draw things in different ways.

Studies

These drawings of hands were made by the artist Albrecht Dürer in the 15th century. For each drawing, the artist had to carefully study what he saw in front of him. We call a drawing like this a "study" because of this.

These drawings would have helped Dürer when he worked on paintings of people.

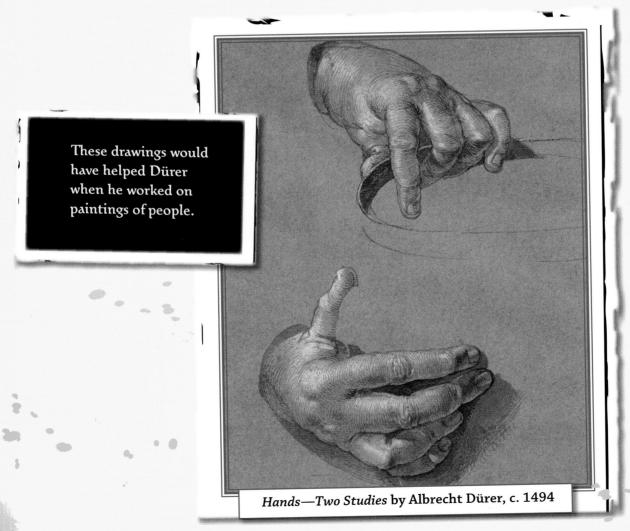

Hands—Two Studies by Albrecht Dürer, c. 1494

Can you see some of the faun's body from the side? Can you also see the faun's face looking straight at you?

Did you know?
Artists start a new study when they are unhappy with the last one or because they need to find out what the subject looks like in different positions. Often these studies are practice for a final piece.

Detail from *Satyr, Faun, and Centaur* by Pablo Picasso, c. 1955

Different views

Pablo Picasso used his experiences of drawing from life to imagine what a **mythological creature** might look like. In this drawing he has created a creature called a faun. Picasso liked to think about what a subject looked like from different angles. He then mixed these up in his work.

Art and Science

Just as Dürer made studies of hands, artists draw studies of other things in nature. If we look very carefully at how something is put together, we can learn how it might work. Leonardo da Vinci is famous for helping us understand the natural world through his detailed drawings. Sometimes he would show the whole subject and then focus on smaller areas in separate drawings. He also sometimes added color.

Floral Study by Leonardo da Vinci, date unknown

Like Dürer, Leonardo sometimes used his drawings to help him paint.

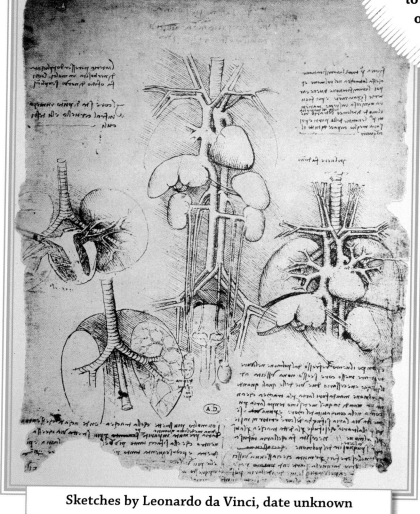

Sketches by Leonardo da Vinci, date unknown

The body

Leonardo da Vinci was allowed to draw various parts of the human
body at hospitals in Italy. The drawing above shows a detailed study of
a human heart and lungs. Sometimes Leonardo would write notes next
to his drawings. The notes around the drawing give more information
about what he saw as he studied the subject. He also drew many
animals, such as cows, birds, monkeys, bears, and frogs.

Tricks of the Trade

Artists sometimes use a piece of equipment called the camera obscura to help them draw. The camera obscura puts an image of a subject onto a sheet of paper or **canvas** so the artist can trace the outline. It is made of a special box, or room. It is large enough for the paper or canvas needed for the finished artwork to hang inside it. On the opposite wall from the paper is a small hole pointing straight at the subject. Light comes through the hole and makes an upside-down image on the paper. The artist traces this image and then turns the paper the right way up.

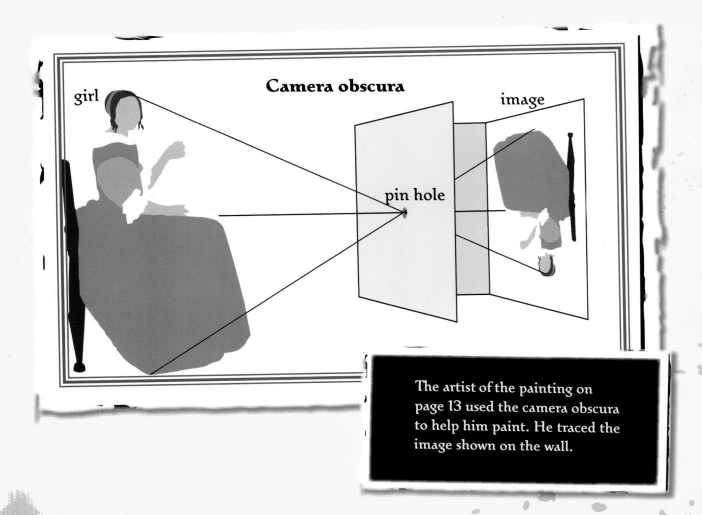

Camera obscura

girl

image

pin hole

The artist of the painting on page 13 used the camera obscura to help him paint. He traced the image shown on the wall.

Vermeer sat in a camera obscura with his back to the young woman and traced around an upside-down image. (See the diagram on page 12.)

Do you think the camera obscura is a clever tool that artists use to help them draw? Or do you think it is cheating?

Soldier with Laughing Girl by Jan Vermeer, c. 1659–60

Then and now

The Dutch painter Jan Vermeer made the painting above in the 17th century. In contemporary art, the British artist David Hockney has used the camera obscura method.

Research Drawings

Many artists use drawings as a way to figure out how their final paintings will look. John Constable would have made many pencil drawings in his sketchbook before making this full-sized painting sketch of his most famous work, *The Hay Wain*.

Study for *The Hay Wain* by John Constable, c. 1821

Because the artist is drawing with paint, a practice picture like this one is still called a sketch.

Constable painted this final painting in his studio. He used his sketches in place of the real scene.

Constable still wanted to make some changes for the final painting. Where has the artist decided to do this? Can you spot any differences between the sketch and the finished painting?

The Hay Wain by John Constable, 1821

The painting shows Flatford Mill in Suffolk, England, where the artist used to play when he was a young boy. Constable would spend hours **sketching** different parts of the scene. He would make individual drawings and small paintings of trees, the cottage, the people, and horse-drawn carts. The cart in the painting carries hay and is called a hay wain. Constable would sketch at different times of the day to show the way the light changed. With all this information he was then able to make the final large painting we see here.

What Are Cartoons?

When we think of cartoons, we think of comic strips or movies. But originally cartoons were full-sized drawings that artists put onto paintings or **tapestries**. People who made stained-glass windows first used cartoons. They made designs for large church windows and then cut them up into sections to be made in smaller parts.

Leonardo da Vinci drew this cartoon as part of his work on a painting, but it was never used. That is why it still exists today.

Virgin and Child with St. Anne and St. John the Baptist by Leonardo da Vinci, 1499

Before painters used cartoons in this way, they drew their designs straight onto a **canvas** or a wall. Drawing a cartoon on paper first was much better. Artists could change their mind more easily, and also their assistants could use the cartoons to draw the designs without the master artist there. This was a big help when artists worked on many projects at the same time.

Most cartoons did not last. When artists put the image of a cartoon onto a wall or canvas, the cartoons were ruined. The artists made small holes on the drawn lines of the cartoon and then brushed powdered charcoal through these holes with a special brush. When the cartoon was removed, the artists joined these dots to make a complete image. Then they could start painting.

Cartoons Today

Mickey Mouse

The word "cartoon" has changed over the years to not simply mean a first-draft drawing. It now also means a comical drawing. Sometimes it can be a series of drawings that make up a story. Mickey Mouse is probably the most famous cartoon character of all time. He was created in 1928 by Walt Disney.

To make an **animation**, an artist needs to make many drawings. These are then filmed one after the other. When they are shown together, it looks like the character is moving. This works just like a flip picture book. Mickey Mouse animated cartoons became popular very quickly. In 1930 Mickey Mouse appeared in comic books, too.

Mickey Mouse comic cover

Compare this Mickey Mouse cartoon with the Leonardo da Vinci cartoon on page 16. They are very different, but can you spot any similarities?

Modern-day cartoon of President George W. Bush

Caricatures

Caricatures are a type of drawing that focuses on a person's features
and makes them seem larger than life. Artists also use caricatures
to tell us something about a person's character. Famous people,
such as politicians and actors, are often the subject of caricatures.
Caricatures can be very funny, but also sometimes quite cruel.

Famous Cartoonists

Ted Seuss, who created the children's Cat in the Hat character, said that he was a doodler at heart. As a student he would doodle away all day. He eventually realized that he wanted to try to make his job drawing cartoons. Many children have enjoyed learning to read with the funny Cat in the Hat and his friends. The rhymes in the books are linked to the pictures, so it is easy to figure out the story from the images as well as from the words.

Dr. Seuss's books have been translated into 15 languages.

The *Mr. Men*

The *Mr. Men* series began in the early 1970s. In 1981 a *Little Miss* series was started, featuring female characters.

The *Mr. Men* characters are all very simple cartoons. Roger Hargreaves drew the *Mr. Men* characters in a way that hints at their name. We call this **symbolism**. Mr. Tickle, for example, has very long arms. Mr. Strong is a hard-angled square shape, and Mr. Daydream's body is based on a cloud.

Comic Books and TV Cartoons

The action hero Superman started as a comic strip and is famous all over the world today. Superman is also in movies and on television. This image is from the original comic strip design. Is it any different from the modern Superman image we know today?

64 PAGES OF ACTION!

ALL IN FULL COLOR

THE COMPLETE STORY OF THE DARING EXPLOITS OF THE ONE AND ONLY SUPERMAN

What is it about the design of Superman that makes him into a superhero? Is it just his clothes? Perhaps the way he stands or the shape of his body also help us think about his special powers.

Superman was one of the first superheroes to appear in U.S. comic books.

Japanese cartoon characters have a style of their own. They are very popular in Japan with all age groups. They can be found in magazines, on TV programs, and in feature-length films.

One very famous cartoon series in Japan was created in a comic book by artist Machiko Hasegawa and has been on Japanese TV since 1969. All the characters are related to the sea. The name of the lead character, Sazae, means a type of shellfish in Japanese. She is a 23-year-old housewife who lives with her parents, younger brother, sister, husband, and baby son. Through the family's daily life, stories are told about Japanese **culture**. Many thousands of people in Japan tune in to catch up with Sazae's family.

Drawing on Walls

These cartoons have been drawn on a wall using spray paint. We call this graffiti. As long as graffiti is created in a place where people are happy to see it, then it can be a very powerful way for people to show how they feel and what is important to them. Some graffiti artists design their own special characters that they use again and again. These act as a type of signature, so people can recognize whose work they are looking at.

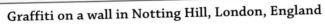

Graffiti on a wall in Notting Hill, London, England

Look at both of these wall pictures. The one above was done recently. The one opposite was drawn thousands of years ago. Why do you think each one was made?

Graffiti is usually against the law. There are different types of graffiti, though. Do you have it around where you live? Is it like the picture above, or do you also see scribbled names and symbols? Or do you have both types? Do you see a difference?

Cave paintings may have simply been decoration. Why else might people have drawn on the walls of caves? Could the drawings have had another purpose?

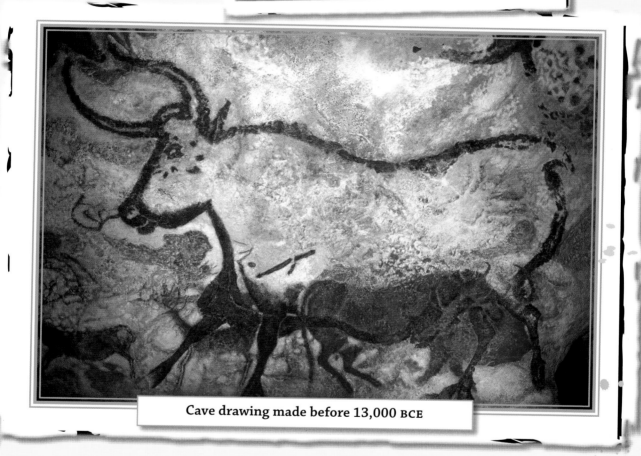

Cave drawing made before 13,000 BCE

People have been drawing on walls for thousands of years. The drawings above were made on cave walls in **prehistoric** times. The materials the people used were very different from the modern graffiti we can see on the opposite page. Instead of spray paint, people drew the outlines of the animals using natural materials like charcoal and chalk. The images were then filled in with colors made from berries, flowers, and even animals' blood.

Drawing Conclusions

In this book we have looked at many reasons why artists practice the art of drawing. We have seen how all artists make drawings at some stage of their work. This can be to figure out how a final design may look, to explore a subject in detail, or to use as a final piece in its own right.

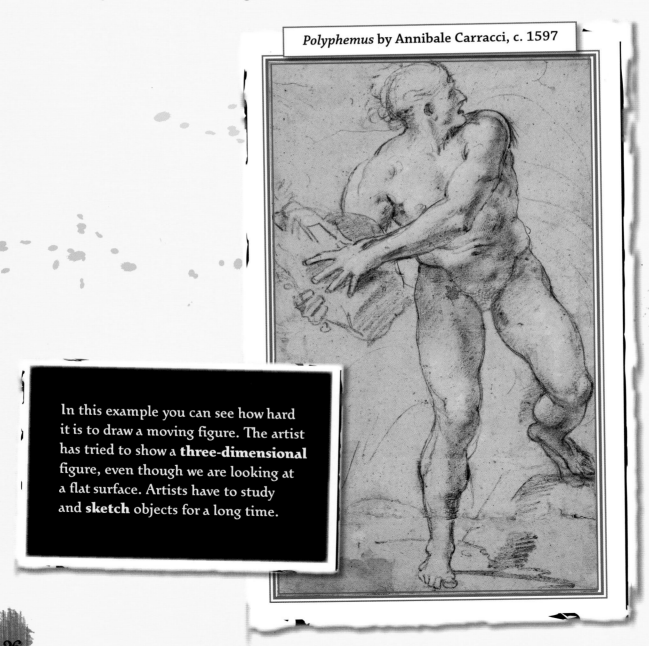

Polyphemus by Annibale Carracci, c. 1597

In this example you can see how hard it is to draw a moving figure. The artist has tried to show a **three-dimensional** figure, even though we are looking at a flat surface. Artists have to study and **sketch** objects for a long time.

Sketch for *The Races* by Edouard Manet, c. 1865

Most drawings are delicate, and many do not survive over time. One way for artists to make their drawings last for a long time is to make an **etching** or **lithograph**. These are drawings made on metal plates or stone tablets. When the drawing is finished, the artist treats the plate or tablet with special chemicals. This wears away the areas where the artist has drawn and makes a plate. This plate can be used to print many examples of the drawing.

Timeline

before 13,000 BCE	**Prehistoric** cave paintings (p. 25)
1452–1519 CE	Leonardo da Vinci (he drew many botanical studies like the one on p. 10)
c. 1494	Albrecht Dürer, *Hands—Two Studies* (p. 8)
c. 1499	Leonardo da Vinci, *Virgin and Child with St. Anne and St. John the Baptist* ("Leonardo Cartoon") (p. 16)
c. 1500	Leonardo da Vinci, *The Heart and the Circulation* (p. 11)
c. 1540	Michelangelo, Study for *The Last Judgment* (p. 4)
c. 1545	Baccio Bandinelli, *Studies of Heads and Arms* (p. 6)
c. 1597–1601	Annibale Carracci, *Polyphemus* (p. 26)
c. 1659–1660	Jan Vermeer, *Soldier with Laughing Girl*—using a camera obscura (p. 13)
1820–1821	John Constable, Study for *The Hay Wain* (p. 14)
c. 1865–1872	Edouard Manet, Sketch for *The Races* (p. 27)
1883–1884	Georges Seurat, *Seated Boy with Straw Hat*, Study for *Bathers at Asnières* (p. 7)
1930	Mickey Mouse comic first printed (p. 18)
1949	Henri Matisse, *Ballet Dancer* (p. 5)
1950s	Dr. Seuss covers first printed (p. 20)
c. 1955	Pablo Picasso, *Satyr, Faun, and Centaur* (p. 9)
1962	First *Spiderman* comic, Stan Lee
c. 1966	Earliest appearance of street graffiti as it is known today. It reached its peak in the early 1980s, but is still popular today.
1969	First appearance of Sazae-san Japanese TV cartoon character (p. 23)
early 1970s	Roger Hargreaves's *Mr. Men* covers first printed (p. 21)

Where to See Drawings

This map shows where some of the artwork in the book can be seen.

① London, England
The National Gallery:
Virgin and Child with St. Anne and St. John the Baptist, Leonardo da Vinci
Sketch for *The Hay Wain*, John Constable
Bathers at Asnières, Georges Seurat
See also: The Cartoon Museum

② Rome, Italy
The Sistine Chapel

③ Brunswick, Germany
Herzog Anton Ulrich Museum: *Soldier with Laughing Girl*, Jan Vermeer

④ New York, New York
Metropolitan Museum of Art:
Faun and Starry Night, Pablo Picasso

⑤ Chicago, Illinois
Art Institute of Chicago:
The Races, Edouard Manet

Glossary

animation   many drawings shown one after the other so that they look like a moving picture

canvas   cloth material that many artists use to paint on

cross-hatching   when an artist draws small lines in one direction and then draws other lines over the top in another direction

culture   customs of a particular time and group of people

discipline   training oneself to become better at something

etching   design scratched onto a metal plate, which is then dipped in acid. The acid eats into the lines on the plate, which can then be used to print lots of copies.

lithograph   type of print made by drawing on a flat stone or metal surface with wax. When ink is added, it sticks to the wax. The stone or metal can then be used to print many copies.

model   person who is the subject of an artwork

mythological creature   creature from a traditional story involving supernatural or imaginary people

prehistoric   from the earliest times, before records of events were made

shading   adding dark and light to a drawing to make it stand out from the page

sketch   roughly make a drawing or painting

symbolism   something that represents something else

tapestry   material with a woven design, usually hung an a wall

three-dimensional (3-D)   having length, width, and depth

tonal   relating to light and shade

Learn More

Books to read

Flux, Paul. *Line and Tone (How Artists Use)*. Chicago: Heinemann Library, 2007.

Spilsbury, Richard. *Cartoons and Animation (Art Off the Wall)*. Chicago: Heinemann Library, 2007.

Spilsbury, Richard. *Comic and Graphic Novels (Art Off the Wall)*. Chicago: Heinemann Library, 2007.

Websites to visit

All about Dr. Seuss—his life and drawings
www.seussville.com

Biography and works of Leonardo da Vinci
www.mos.org/leonardo

The Metropolitan Museum of Art's website for kids
www.metmuseum.org/explore/museumkids.htm

The National Gallery of Art's website for kids
www.nga.gov/kids/kids.htm

Index

accuracy 5
animations 18
art museums 29

Bandinelli, Baccio 6
blood 25

camera obscura 12–13
canvas 12, 17
caricatures 19
Carracci, Annibale 26
cartoons 16–23, 24
cave paintings 25
chalk 25
charcoal 17, 25
color 10, 21, 25
comic strips 22
comical drawings 18–21
Constable, John 14–15
cross-hatching 6

discipline 9
Disney, Walt 18
drawing from life 4, 5, 7
Dürer, Albrecht 7

first-draft drawings 17, 18

graffiti 24

Hargreaves, Roger 21
Hasegawa, Machiko 23
Hockney, David 13
human body 4, 5, 6, 7, 11, 26

Japanese cartoons 23

landscapes 15
Leonardo da Vinci 10–11, 16
light sources 8
lithographs 27

Manet, Edouard 27
Matisse, Henri 5
Michelangelo Buonarotti 4
Mickey Mouse 18
models 4
movement 26
Mr. Men 21
mythological creatures 9

natural world 10, 11, 15, 25

paint 14
Picasso, Pablo 9
prehistoric art 25

Seurat, Georges 8
Seuss, Ted 20
shading 6, 8
Sistine Chapel 4
sketching 5, 14, 15, 26
stained-glass windows 16
studies 7, 9, 10
Superman 22
symbolism 21, 24

tapestries 16
three-dimensional (3-D) drawings 6, 8, 26
timeline 28
tonal drawings 6
tones 6, 8

Vermeer, Jan 13